My Moving Workbook

This Workbook Belongs To:

Moving Forward Together :
An Interactive Workbook for Kids on the Move

Copyright © 2023 by Dylan Meikle & Anissa Zotos

First print edition September 2023

Illustrations by Sakshi Mangal - https://www.sakshimangal.com
Book design by Veronica Scott - https://reedsy.com/veronica-scott

ISBN 979-8-9878167-2-1 (hardcover)
ISBN 979-8-9878167-1-4 (paperback)
ISBN 979-8-9878167-3-8 (ebook)

Published by Macquarie Publishing Pty Ltd, Canberra, Australia

movingforwardkids.com

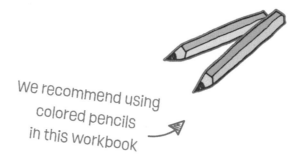

We recommend using colored pencils in this workbook

Moving Forward Together

An Interactive Workbook for Kids on the Move

Dylan Meikle & Anissa Zotos

Art by Sakshi Magal

"One day, life begins to change.

We learn we will be leaving,

and deep inside we begin to prepare."

Third Culture Kids: The Experience of Growing Up Among Worlds
Pollock, Van Reken & Pollock (2010)

*Pages with this icon are best discussed
with an adult to maximise your child's
understanding and growth.*

Dear Family on The Move,

Relocating, whether domestically or internationally, can be a major life upheaval that requires cognitive and emotional processing. It's important for both children and adults to collect memories, reflect, and express their feelings of hope and loss in order to make meaning of the changes they're facing.

Moving can be a challenging experience, but it also presents an opportunity for families to come together and move forward with shared optimism. To help you and your child muster the social and emotional energy that relocation requires, we've created this interactive workbook.

This workbook includes activities and support to help you and your child before, during, and after your relocation. Some of the pages can be completed independently, while others are best completed with the guidance of an adult such as a parent, teacher, school counselor, or grandparent.

Encouraging your child to draw, write, add photos, and talk about the activities in this book will help them prepare for the transition and arrive ready to engage with their new school, new friends, and new life.

We wish you happiness and success during your relocation.

Warmly,
Dylan and Anissa

My Family Is Moving

I am _____ years old.

I lived in _____ for _____ years.

I went to my current school for _____ years.

Something that excites me about moving is

_____

Draw a symbol or famous building representing the place you currently live

Draw a symbol or famous building found in the place you are moving to

Life At School

My FAVORITE things at school are

Circle things you like, or draw your own

My FIRST FRIEND at school was

_____

My BEST friends now are

_____

_____

_____

_____

The PLACE I like best at school is

_____

_____

_____

My Home

I have LIVED in my home for _____ years.

Some SPECIAL OCCASIONS my family shared there were

_____

_____

Things I LIKE MOST about my home are

_____

_____

_____

All About Me

Draw YOURSELF or add a photo

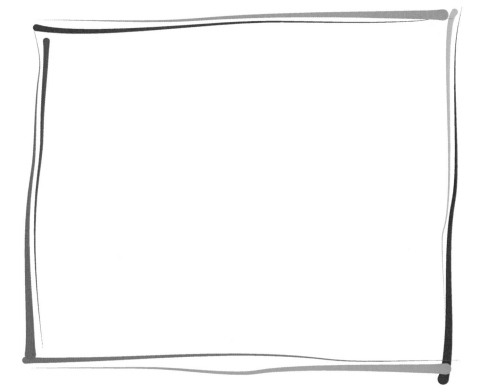

Languages I speak

_____

_____

_____

Draw FLAGS that are important to you

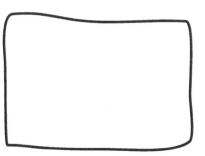

My Journey so Far...

On the map, DRAW and LINK the places where you
have previously lived and traveled to

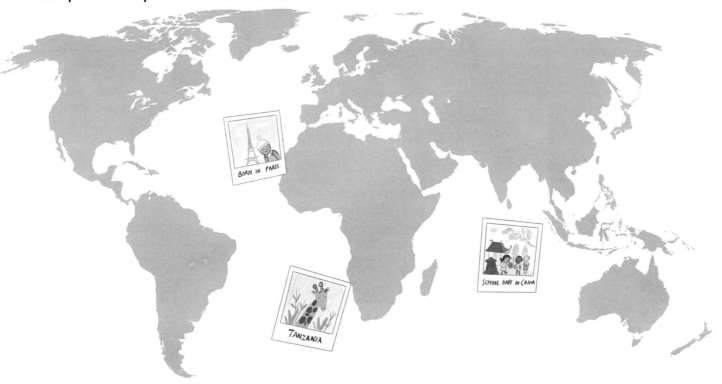

What major FAMILY EVENTS can you add to this timeline?

then...   now...   moving
                                         forwards...

My Favorite Things...
(Right Now)

Draw or write answers above the flowers

What's your favorite thing
to do in your neighborhood?

What hobby or
sport do you love?

Who's your
favorite teacher?

What's your favorite
place to go on weekends?

My Strengths

My friends think I am...

I'm really good at...

My parents say I'm...

My teachers say I'm...

When I play I love to play with...

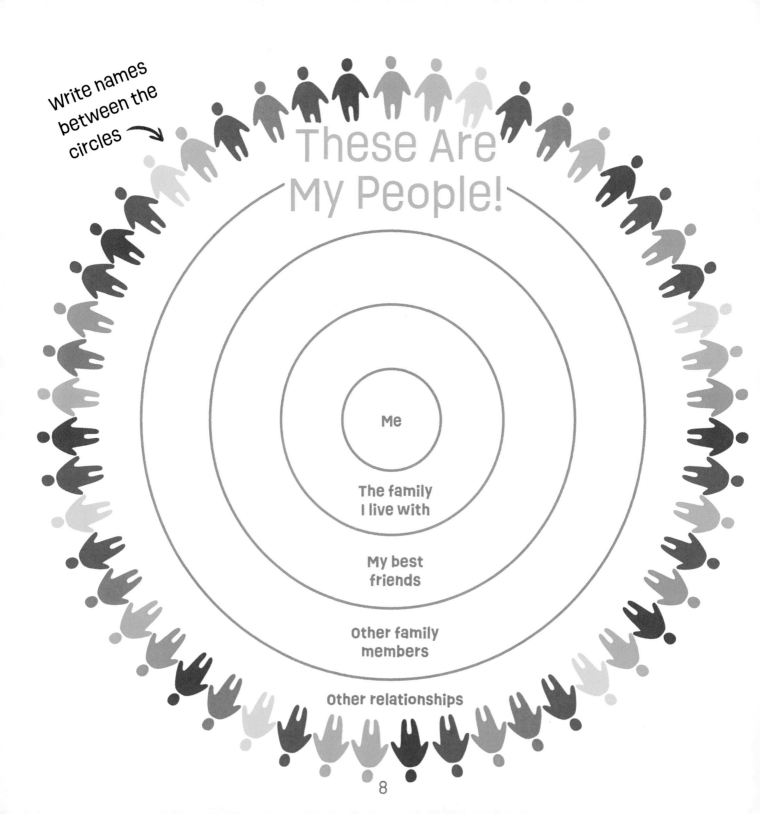

Write names between the circles →

These Are
My People!

Me

The family
I live with

My best
friends

Other family
members

Other relationships

8

Moving Makes Me Feel...

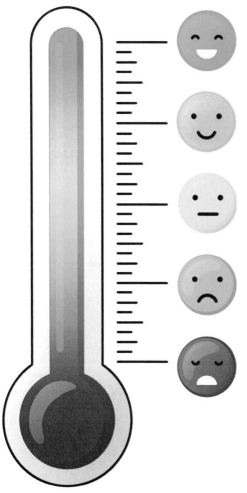

Do you ever feel big emotions when things change? Moving can be exciting, but it can also be stressful.

Lots of kids feel a mix of emotions when they move. Maybe you're feeling happy, nervous and sad all at once!

Use the emojis to CIRCLE how you're feeling

Are you feeling calm and collected like the green zone, or do you feel anxious and hot like the red zone?

Use this thermometer to track how you're feeling over time.

Draw your own CREATIVE EMOJIS too!

9

What Do Kids Usually Worry About When They Move?

Moving to a new place can be an EXCITING ADVENTURE, but it's also okay to feel worried or scared. Many kids have questions and concerns about what their new home and school will be like.

Here are some common worries kids have:

What will my new SCHOOL be like?

What will my new HOUSE be like?

Will my new school have too much HOMEWORK?

Will my friends FORGET about me?

Will I miss my OLD FRIENDS?

Remember, it's okay to have worries and questions. Talking to your family and friends can help you feel better and make the transition to your new home a little easier.

Worry Bubbles

It's normal to have worries, and it can be helpful to write them down to get them out of your head. Use the worry bubbles to jot down any concerns you have.

TOGETHER

Let's "POP!" Some Worry Bubbles!

You can do this by thinking about your strengths. You are a STRONG KID, and trusting in those strengths can help you feel better. It's always a good idea to talk things through with an adult you trust, too.

For example:
My friend Finley, who is 9 years old...

Sometimes Finley worries, "What if I don't make any new friends?"

But Finley has many strengths that make them a great friend. Their friends think they are friendly, fun, and caring.

By remembering all their strengths Finley feels more confident about being the kind of kid that can make new friends.

Go back and read your strengths on page #7. A cool kid like you will make new friends too!

Even when we're really good at something, like being a friend, we can still feel worried about new things.

It takes time to meet new people and make friends, but it will happen eventually.

In the meantime, Finley can "POP!" some worry bubbles and remember how awesome they are. Finley is kind and funny, and that's why people like to be around them. They should trust that everything will work out.

The Power Of "Yet"

Do you have worries about moving to a new place?

You might think of questions, like what your new house will be like, if you'll be able to get a hamster, or who your new teacher will be.

It's normal to think about these things, but you don't need to worry all the time.

If you trust in your strengths, you can "POP!" some of those worry bubbles. And it's okay if you don't have all the answers **yet**. It takes time for families to work out all the details when moving to a new country.

You can tell yourself, "I don't know about that yet, and that's okay!"

TOGETHER

Some problems are for adults to worry about, not kids. So don't worry too much about things you can't control. FOCUS ON BEING A KID AND ON HAVING FUN!

13

Change Is a Normal Part Of Life

Even when things change, YOUR FAMILY LOVES YOU and your strengths can help you thrive!

It's normal for things to change. You grow and change, and your family does too.

But even when things are different, your family still loves you just as much.

And you still have all the strengths that make you special, like being kind, funny, or smart.

Houses Change But Some Things Don't

TOGETHER

There are different places to live all over the world.

Big and small - apartments and houses.

When we move house some THINGS CHANGE - but some things STAY THE SAME.

Think about the things that won't really change when you move and the things that will be different.

Different - Good!

Things that won't change

Different - Maybe Not Good

You Care About People - and It's Time to Tell Them!

➡ Who do you think about the most when you think about moving?

➡ Write them a special message on the POSTCARD below.

➡ Start your message with **"You are special to me because..."** and show them this page!

➡ It's important to let people know they're special before you say goodbye. Who else can you write a note to?

Create a list of special people you want to say goodbye to before you move.

These could include FRIENDS, FAMILY MEMBERS, NEIGHBORS, COACHES, TEACHERS, BABYSITTERS, or anyone else who has made an impact on your life.

Ask your parents for help in identifying people in the community who are important to say goodbye to, such as SHOPKEEPERS, LIBRARIANS, or other local figures. It's important to show appreciation for these special people and let them know how much they mean to you before you move.

Write your list here

Saying Goodbye to Places

It's important to say goodbye to places that have become special to you and your family before you move.

Here are some things you can do to make the most of your time:

Make a list of your favorite places, like parks or museums, and visit them one last time.

Think about the restaurants you love and plan to eat at before you leave.

Make a list of activities you enjoy, like playing mini-golf or going to the movies, and try to do them before you move.

By taking time to visit these places and do these things, you can create SPECIAL MEMORIES that will stay with you even after you've moved away.

Places Are Special

Ask your family to visit your
FAVORITE PLACES one last time
and say "goodbye for now!"

I said goodbye to
my favorite DONUTS!

my bedroom

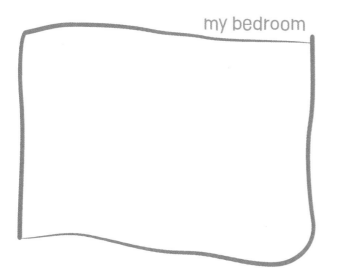

Draw or
add a photo:

my classroom

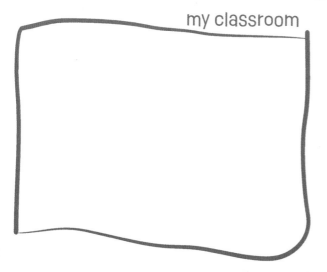

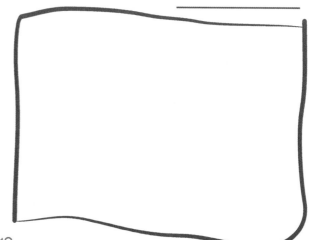

19

You Can't Take It All With You

Sometimes when families move, they can't take everything with them. It's okay to feel sad about LEAVING THINGS BEHIND, like toys, bikes, books, or pets. You can draw pictures or attach photos of those things you won't be able to bring with you.

It's normal to feel a sense of loss when we say goodbye to something we care about.

TOGETHER

Remember to talk to someone you trust about how you're feeling.

Sharing your emotions with others can help you feel better.

Which Special Books or Toys Are You Planning on Taking?

My parents say my rock collection is too big and heavy to take with me. But I love it! What should I do?

It's tough to leave something you love behind, but taking photos of your rock collection is a great way to remember it.

You could also consider giving your rocks to a friend who loves rocks too! That way, you can make someone else happy while still feeling connected to your collection.

And when you get to your new house, you can start a new rock collection and make new memories.

Why Is Your Family Moving?

Understanding WHY your family is moving can help you feel more comfortable with the change. Talk to your parents or caregivers and ask them questions like:

➡ Why are we moving?

➡ What are some of the benefits of moving that you are looking forward to?

➡ Does your job have something to do with the move?

➡ Why is now the right time to move?

This can help you understand the reasons behind the move and feel more prepared for the changes that are coming.

TOGETHER

WHY

Write some notes here

Your Family Needs To Help Each Other

Moving can be a big job, but everyone in your family can help out and make the process easier! Imagine you have a magic crystal ball that lets you discover ways to help each person in your family.

Draw a picture of each family member and write down how you can help them during the move.

For example, you could clean your room and donate old toys and books to help your dad.

Your baby brother might need someone to play with while your parents are busy, so you could spend time with him. Your dog might need extra walks because of the changes, and you can help by taking him out more often.

And you can make things easier for your parents by avoiding fights with your siblings during this busy time. Don't forget to talk to your parents about what you need too!

Me? I just need this ball.

Ask Your Teachers to Write
a Farewell Message

Some people like to leave a LITTLE SOMETHING of themselves behind when they move. Somehow it feels special to think that in our old house or school there is a SPECIAL SECRET connection that we hid away!

Some children find special SMOOTH ROCKS and write a message on them with markers - and then hide them or bury them in their BACKYARD or PLAYGROUND.

Some families hide a little 'TIME CAPSULE' with a couple of special items inside. They might hide it in their house on the day that they move out!

TALK TO YOUR FAMILY ABOUT THIS IDEA.

You can also think about giving a SMALL GIFT to a friend to celebrate a special friendship. The gift doesn't have to be too big - in fact it is better to give a small and MEANINGFUL item.

If you are leaving any family members behind make sure you really connect with them too - tell them how SPECIAL they are before you move.

Messages From Friends

Researching Your Destination

Gathering information about a new destination helps us feel more RELAXED and EXCITED about the adventure ahead.

Ask your family to research with you and use ONLINE RESOURCES like GOOGLE EARTH to explore the area and learn about its unique features.

If you know your new school's name, check if they have a website for more information. If not, research the great things your new city has to offer, such as LANDMARKS, ATTRACTIONS, or CULTURAL EXPERIENCES.

By doing so, you can build excitement for your upcoming move and feel MORE PREPARED.

COOL DISCOVERIES I MADE ABOUT MY NEW CITY AND COUNTRY:

This Is Where I'm Going

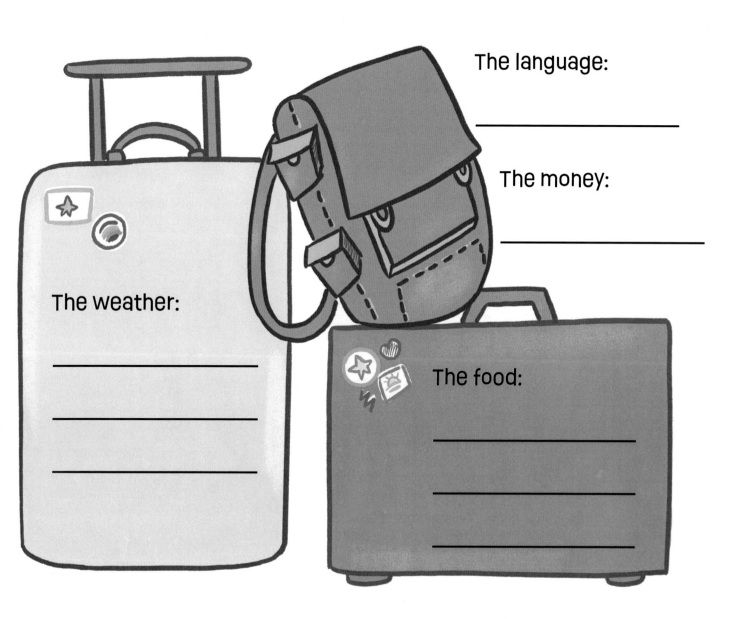

The language:

_____

The money:

_____

The weather:

_____

_____

_____

The food:

_____

_____

_____

I'm Happy to Leave This Behind!

When we move sometimes we are glad to get a break from some things. What are you happy to LEAVE BEHIND?

Some kids don't like lots of traffic!

Some kids notice too much air pollution or trash where they live!

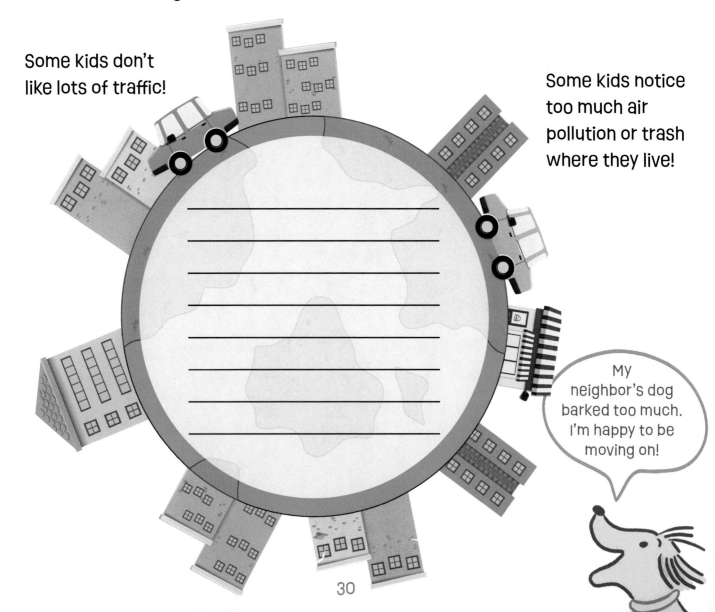

My neighbor's dog barked too much. I'm happy to be moving on!

I'm Looking Forward to...

Good things are on their way!

Write your HOPES for your new place here

My Arrival Plan

Making new friends can be scary, but it can also be FUN! Here are some ideas to help you make NEW FRIENDS:

1. Be BRAVE and say "hi" or "can I play?" to other kids at your new school.

2. Join a club or activity that you enjoy. You'll meet other kids who like the SAME THINGS as you.

3. When you move into your new house, invite someone over for a PLAYDATE!

4. Ask your parents if they can help you CONNECT with other kids in your new place before you move. If they can, send them a message and say "hi."

Remember, making friends takes time and effort, but it's WORTH IT! You'll have someone to play with, share your toys with, and have fun together.

My friendship strengths:

To use my strengths
to make friends I will:

Your Family Is Special and Unique

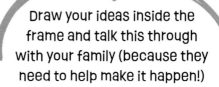

Families do SPECIAL THINGS together that make them happy, like watching movies on Saturday nights, going on BIKE RIDES every Sunday, or having a SPECIAL DINNER on Fridays. These are called FAMILY TRADITIONS, and they help families bond and make great memories.

When families move to a new home, they might not be able to do their traditions in the same way. But it's important to try and keep them going! You can think of new ways to do your traditions, like finding a NEW PARK to PLAY SOCCER in or MAKING POPCORN in a new kitchen.

It's a good idea to talk to your family about your traditions and how you can keep doing them. You can DRAW your ideas and share them with your family. When everyone works together, it makes it easier to keep your family traditions going, even in a NEW HOME.

Draw your ideas inside the frame and talk this through with your family (because they need to help make it happen!)

New Friendships Take Time

Imagine a beautiful pearl necklace.

Just like how a pearl necklace is made by adding each pearl to a string one at a time, friendships are made by getting to know someone and SPENDING TIME TOGETHER.

It takes time to create a beautiful necklace, and it takes time to create a STRONG FRIENDSHIP. But every day that you try to make friends with someone is like adding one more pearl to your necklace.

So be patient and keep trying, and soon you'll have a beautiful friendship that you'll treasure forever!

One day at a time!

Moving Can Feel Like a Whirlwind

People I miss:

Things I miss doing:

Things that I like here:

Things that are weird here:

My New School

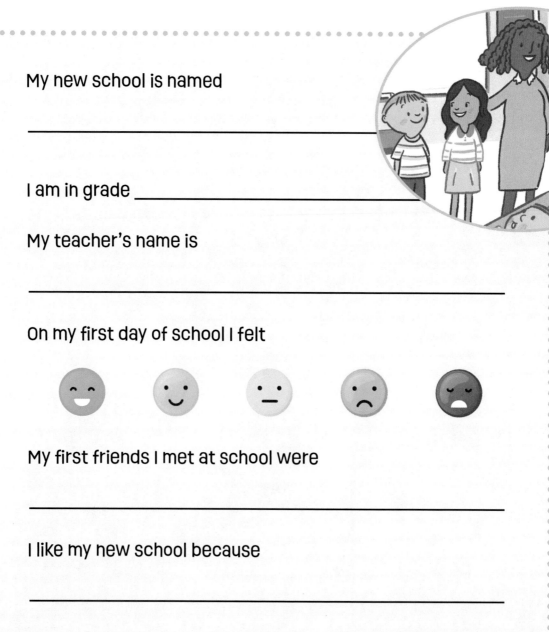

My new school is named

_____

I am in grade _____

My teacher's name is

_____

On my first day of school I felt

My first friends I met at school were

_____

I like my new school because

_____

My New Home

Welcome to your NEW HOME! What is it like?

My new address _____

_____

Draw a little map or picture of your new bedroom:

I like my new home because

Wherever I go, my home is where my family is.

MOVINGFORWARDKIDS.COM

Continue the journey at **movingforwardkids.com** to:

- Access complimentary lesson plans designed to help counselors and teachers seamlessly integrate Moving Forward and Moving Forward Together into their professional practice.

- Explore thought-provoking conversation starters and key questions to facilitate meaningful discussions about Moving Forward in both home and school settings.

- Discover valuable moving tips, useful links, and more!

ABOUT THE AUTHORS

Anissa Zotos

Anissa believes that the best thing about moving countries is the opportunity to meet new friends from all walks of life. With her wealth of knowledge and compassionate approach, she is dedicated to helping families navigate the challenges of moving with ease and confidence. Anissa has served learning communities across the United States and the world, including international schools in Scotland and Vietnam. She is a counselor, student support specialist, and animal lover who is always *"moving forward"* with her globetrotting cat.

Dylan Meikle

Dylan thinks the best thing about moving to a new country is getting to experience new languages and cultures while munching local cuisine. An Australian, he has lived and worked in China, Vietnam and Singapore with his two delightful daughters, wonderful wife and darling dog. He is a teacher, counselor and Dean of Students.